CANDLEWICK PRESS

First US edition 2022. Library of Congress Catalog Card Number pending. ISBN 978-1-5362-2046-9. This book was typeset in HVD Bodedo and Hammersmith One. The illustrations were done in mixed media.
Candlewick Press, 99 Dover Street, Somerville, Massachusetts 02144. www.candlewick.com.
Printed in Heshan, Guangdong, China. 21 22 23 24 25 26 LEO 10 9 8 7 6 5 4 3 2 1

FIND OUT ABOUT
Animal Babies

Martin Jenkins

illustrated by

Jane McGuinness

There are millions of different kinds of animals in the world.
They eat all sorts of different things and live in all sorts of places.
But there's one thing they all do: they all have babies!
There are lots of different kinds of babies and lots of different
ways of raising them. Here are a few. . .

Some animals have **BIG** babies.

A blue whale is the biggest baby in the world. It is about twenty-five feet (more than seven meters) long and weighs three tons when it is born.

Some have babies that are small . . .

Kangaroo babies are born tiny — less than one inch (2.5 centimeters) long.
The baby crawls through its mother's fur to reach her pouch, where it stays
warm and safe, and grows and grows and grows.

not that they stay
small for long.

Some animals look after their
babies for years and years.

6

Young male African elephants stay with their mothers until they are at least ten years old. Females usually don't leave at all!

And some don't look after them at all.

A female sea turtle comes out of the ocean to lay her eggs on a beach.
She covers them with sand and goes back to the sea, leaving the eggs to hatch
by themselves weeks later.

Some animals have babies that look just like them . . .

Most lizards lay eggs. Many have babies that don't change shape very much as they grow.

and some don't.

Butterflies start life as eggs, which hatch and release caterpillars. Eventually a caterpillar turns into something called a chrysalis. Inside the chrysalis, the caterpillar's body breaks down and regrows as a butterfly.

Some animals keep their babies in
very strange places: in their mouths . . .

A female mouth-brooding cichlid fish lays eggs that she keeps in her mouth until they hatch. Once released, the babies leave her mouth to feed but dart back in if danger threatens.

in their stomachs . . .

A female gastric-brooding frog (sadly now extinct) gobbled down her eggs and kept them in her stomach, where they hatched into tadpoles. After they turned into tiny frogs, she vomited them up!

or in little holes in the skin on their backs.

The eggs of Suriname toads sink into their mother's back as soon as she has laid them. Each one hatches a tadpole that then becomes a baby toad, which swims away when it's ready.

And some leave them in someone
else's home.

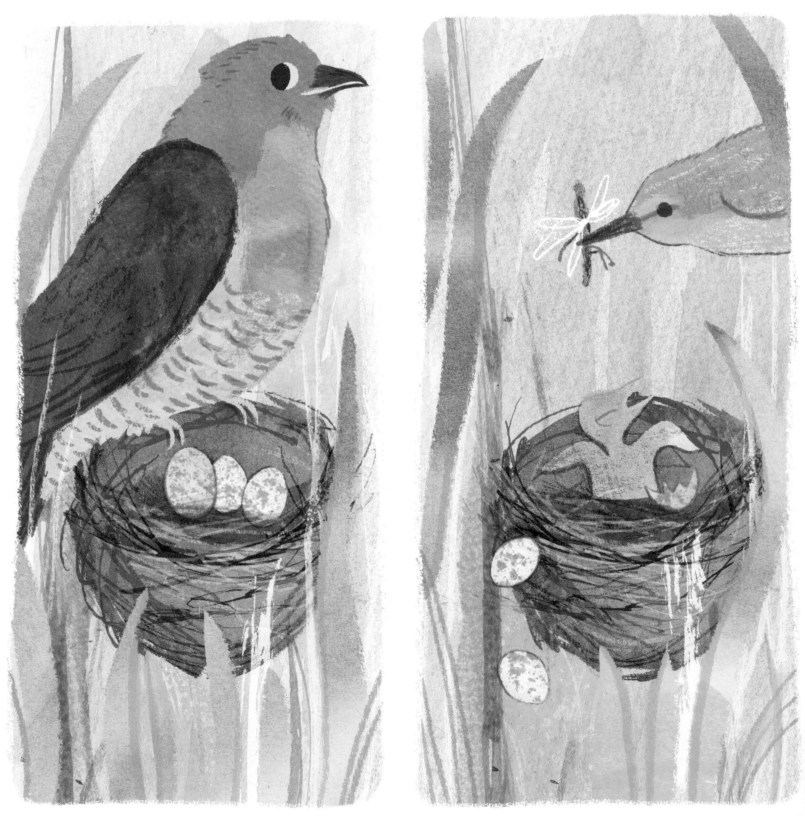

A female cuckoo lays her egg in the nest of another kind of bird, such as a warbler.
The baby cuckoo hatches and quickly pushes any of the warbler's own eggs or babies
out of the nest. The parent warblers think the cuckoo baby is their own, and feed it
and feed it and feed it!

Some animals get together in huge groups to have their babies—the more the merrier!

More than half a million lesser flamingos all nest together at one lake in Tanzania in East Africa. That's a lot of flamingos!

And some have their babies
all alone.

20

A leopard mother hides herself away in a quiet den to have her babies. Their eyes are closed when they are born and don't open for four or five days.

So many ways of bringing up babies, and all with the chance that when they're grown . . .

the babies will have babies
of their own!

Chimpanzees can live to be forty or older and usually have their first baby when they are fourteen or fifteen years old. Quite a few of them are grandparents and some of them are great-grandparents!

More About Animals and Their Babies

Most animals, like birds, most fish, and insects, have babies by laying eggs. The mother grows the eggs inside her body and lays them when they're ready. Some eggs, like frog spawn, are soft and wobbly. Others, like birds' eggs, have a hard shell. Sometimes the mother builds a nest to keep the eggs safe. Sometimes she doesn't. Inside each egg a miniature baby grows. Eventually the egg breaks open and the new baby emerges into the world.

Some animals, including humans, whales, leopards, chimpanzees, and many more, don't lay eggs but have live babies instead. The baby is often born small and helpless. The mother makes milk to feed it. Babies born this way sometimes take quite a long time to grow up.

Not all baby animals survive. Many get eaten by other animals, or can't find enough food of their own. Eventually though, if they're lucky, some grow big enough to have their own babies—and everything starts all over again!

INDEX